My Neighborhood

by Lana Rios
illustrated by Amy Loeffler

PEARSON

Scott
Foresman

Editorial Offices: Glenview, Illinois • Parsippany, New Jersey • New York, New York
Sales Offices: Needham, Massachusetts • Duluth, Georgia • Glenview, Illinois
Coppell, Texas • Ontario, California • Mesa, Arizona

Come see my neighborhood.

See the people who live and work here.

Many people go to shops.

I wave to Sam when we pass his shop.

Many people play in the park.

People pitch balls and use bats.

Many people ride the bus.

I wave to Mike as he gets out.

We see Miss Hines as we ride the bus.

She rides a horse and keeps us safe.

I like my neighborhood.

It is a busy place that is full of people!